HOW
NOT TO KILL
GOVERNMENT LEADERS

Stephen Lawrence was born in Adelaide, and
works for the South Australian government. His
fiction and poetry has won or been shortlisted for
twenty Australian literary awards since 1993, and
has been published in the US, Canada, Denmark
and Romania. This is his third collection of poetry.

HOW

NOT TO KILL

GOVERNMENT LEADERS

poems by

Stephen Lawrence

Wakefield
Press

Wakefield Press
Box 2266
Kent Town
South Australia 5071

First published 2002

Cover design and illustration by Julian Smith
Designed and typeset by Gina Inverarity
Printed and bound by Hyde Park Press, Adelaide

National Library of Australia
Cataloguing-in-publication entry

Lawrence, Stephen.
How not to kill government leaders: poems.

ISBN 1 86254 571 5.

I. Title.

A821.3

Promotion of this book has been assisted
by the South Australian Government
through Arts South Australia.

Publication of this book was assisted by the
Commonwealth Government through the
Australia Council, its arts funding and advisory body.

I shall whisper
Heavenly labials in a world of gutturals.

Wallace Stevens

BY THE SAME AUTHOR

CONTENTS

The Lung Print ("black holes herniate the universe")

The Ammonite Stairwell
("eating the toilet bowl in the gingerbread house")

The Lip Abacus
("ankle-deep in the Santos-blue river, unreeling")

THE
LUNG
PRINT

("black holes herniate the universe")

FLESH MADE WISDOM

1. Ontogeny

The Hydroid. The Flatworm.
The Echinoderm.
The Mollusc. The Vertebrate.

Before I wake
My cells have reviewed evolution,
Have visited all time. My self congeals;

A platter of cells knot into a spinal tube.

Then my brain becomes a novelty balloon
At the end of a busker's bike pump.

Baker's dough rising, knuckle-dimpled.

I am a shark, gills kneading,
An elongated, marine awareness.

The Fish. The Amphibian.
The Reptile.
The Bird. The Mammal.

My thoughts fill and fold out alarmingly.
Oxygenated, encephalated, chains of neurones
Wrinkling into every edge of their cavity.

A puffy endoderm cramps into the skull.

This bladder of awareness, this cerebral hemisphere
Perches awkwardly at the crest of my spine.

I have learnt all I could from the past.

Now my outer layers, my birth-damp receptors,
Await information from the world.

2. Perception

Exterioception. Proprioception.
Interoception. I race to know.

Sky breathes its messages. Violet.
Wraith tears. Net. Wind timbre.

I smell rain. It tastes gold.
It is gold. I think it's raining.

It is raining. The beat of wet fades.
Rain stops. Gold stops. Occipital

Vision. Temporal sound. Parietal
Tactility. Prefrontal: the future.

Blue and grey bloats my hearing
As fatigued yellow recharges sodium pumps;

Photochemical pit-stop, resensitising
Ionic spark-points, charging synapses

Habituated, depleted by steadily transducing
The tastes, the melody of our shaded world.

Rain inhaled flowers, flushes watercolour—
A culture in a Petrie dish—diffuses cool

Seeping around the gut: preconscious
Thought humming into cells.

The air exhales again. I smell gold.
I feel rain. Aureolean feathers.

I know rain. I see meaning,
Touch it and drink.

3. Knowledge

I read. I work. I study. I live. I am.

Input sprays electrons and macromolecules
In watercolour washes around the lobes—
A bath of neurotransmitters: acetylcholine,
Noradrenaline, dopamine, serotonin.

They scurry—in seconds their peripheries will fray,
Their cores decay—riding the Potassium-Sodium exchange
Jostling with other memory-krill—on the way
Shedding atoms, chips and flakes of themselves.

Some loosen and dissipate in this volcanic lake.
Some do not dissolve but firm up, find likely sites, settle.
In the furnace of being, awareness presents as cooler nodes,
Sunspots, precarious rafts—scum, topmost froth—

Residues, neurochemical, on the tips of axons,
Insinuating beneath the skin of neurones—
Knuckling dendritic routes, cataract ghost-colonies
    on nuclei,
Engram-burrs, resident memory-traces on microsurfaces.

The hippocampus, at retrieval, gathers these buds,
Cartilaginous humps, scar tissue-flowers—decodes
    and aligns,
Deep-processes the tiny wounds into recall,
    into knowledge.
Reference memory. Episodic memory. Semantic memory.

Output. I speak. I write. I think. I am incarnate.

PELICAN-CHILD

it inhales, and the changeling turns
in comfortable sleep
umbilical tongue the pillow

under the beak's flaking-rock shield
entrapped in the fish-salt uterus
buoyed and floating amongst warm odours

the child from its snug capsule
feels tickling surges of oxygen
brighten the blood cells

a belch of cod breath awakens him
part boy part fish part bird
greets and mingles with the outside gases

READING ALOUD

Every book is filled with gods,
clustered around typeface (language's
teeth), households inside each letter,
gardens spread through the white syntax.

Finger-shadows watermark yellow;
shaken loose by turning mothwing pages,
motes, pulled into the air by reading,
are rendered, deified by being named.

Born in meaning, words
are the loudspeakers for synapses,
congealing around text, pixels,
tufted fonts, masticating language.

The child feels the gods' guardian auras,
sees these creatures of revelation,
hears slashes of descriptive colour
spreading soft paint on wet paper.

GEORGIA AT ELEVEN

playing so seriously
at being a child

her pudgy sweetness
in hormone denial

tenderly responsible
for the whole world

SKIN GAME

I had heard that Sophie's step-father
drank his thick anger and power
bottle by fiery bottle.

She crunched towards me
with spindle-shanked bravado,
across torsos of bark—

through this grey skin field
of paper-dry tubes,
curled naked and tight.

Her breast-nubs quivered
all the way to the tree,
causing me sudden sweet, damp pain.

At thirteen, all my fears and my friends
were measured in growth-rings.
Should I show her the new quiff in my armpit?

We squatted between root-paddles
that fanned from the bulbous trunk.
It was the secret place

on the hill near our houses,
where we talked of sinful things:
smoking, theft, arson.

"Ow's your mumman dad?"
Sophie's face bruised into a grin—even at eleven,
she pulled the edges of her mouth down to smile.

She produced two paper matches,
split them with her soiled nails,
from club-foot to red neck.

"Win shown me." (Her new dad,
sprawled, burping hops and fish
at their kitchen table,

showing dirty tricks with thick fingers
to his new girl, amongst wet newspapers,
stained napkin fans and rattling bottles.)

Two spreadeagled peg-soldiers,
small stick-children
awaiting their fate—

placed one upon the other
on a flat stone
decorated with fern-fossil doilies.

She hitched up her skirt
to get at its pocket-pleat,
wriggled her fist in there.

I thought I glimpsed
a tiny grey tongue, a black tuft—
and ached and tingled some more.

Sophie flipped open a matchbook
like a little phone, about to
transmit a message from the battle-zone.

The knobby trunk above us
shucked off a brittle shard of skin,
sent it rattling onto a root nearby.

Next to two sad, furry stumps
she wrenched a third match, struck it.
It flared shockingly.

The prone figures' heads went 'fishfish'
touched by the burning match,
and sprayed a grey, stone flower graffiti-black.

When their bodies caught—all leg—
the limbs arched and twined
knotting and humping in agony, aflame.

Sophie snorted dirtily, "Ar, arh, arf."
She looked at me.
"That's your daddun mum. Fuckin."

I watched the varicose limbs flounder, curl
and shrink in slow breaststroke kicks,
and freeze up in death;

nubs of flame
flickered out at the toe-tips,
replaced with a dab of smoke.

Then I looked up at her quivering eye.
She knew secrets I didn't. Sins of torture.
Giving a downward smile—

happiness inverted—
she bolted away, bare legs paddling,
through a shatter of bark.

Now I knew that Sophie was, if not ready,
then prepared. She would divulge.
She would skin herself for me.

WALLET

My boy writes his own business cards:
Name, address, phone, fax, mobile, hotmail,
Raichu in one corner trims to ticket size,
Slips his spreading network into pockets,
Into the card slots of an auxiliary wallet—
Bark-coloured, full-grain Merino leather,
Security nylon loop with popper enclosure—
Slyly palmed from dad's study drawer.

A boy stands in a South Bronx vestibule—
Reaches for his pocket. Charcoal-black:
The colour of a semiautomatic.
Eager to define himself to the people
Of his new country, the West Indian boy
Capered to the embroidery of 41 gunshots
(Embossed by 19). One bullet tunnelled
Up his leg—so pathology tells us—
To nudge his wallet back into his hand.
"Look. Here I am. This is me. After all."

My boy flips his wallet like a police badge
("Where's the gun! Where's the gun!"),
Parades his freshly-minted ID, its formation
A hormonal imperative, adding value—
A serious wood-brown snapdragon, ribbed,
Four card slots, dual note compartments—
Partitioning his brain's growth
Into coin purse and plastic windows.

AU and PB

To me, poetry is a flare of burning gas,
Straight from the jet—blocked from view by
Two carefully placed rugby shoulders
Shielding the back bench with redblack stripes—
Its aura flavoured by the fear (from peers
Apocryphal) that this hissing flame could
Feed back into its pipes and explode the building.

Poetry can thrill and boil, change colour,
Rise fizzing, overflow the rigid tube—
Obeying its arcane logic, firing the mind
With light speed, probabilities, electron clouds.

To them, poetry is porridge and sodden black toast,
A '30s soup-kitchen, Elizabethan fopperies, rotten fruit.
My love douses their interest, my pedantic enthusiasm
Alienates them from the fire's heart. They snore
And fart and guffaw, imaginations circling a scrum
   of protons.

Colleagues from hard subjects use me as litmus:
Science comes to English when the issue is absconding.
If poetry day falls on Chem test day
Male absentees need a rock-solid excuse;
At those times, my soft classes grow bigger and rowdier.
My golden thoughts fall mush-grey and plum-brown.
I turn pink with shame.

BOYS IN PAIN

With bolts of Bones, that fetter'd stands
In feet; and manacled in Hands. . .
A Soul hung up, as 'twere, in Chains
Of Nerves, and Arteries, and Veins.
(*A Dialogue between the Soul and Body*—Andrew Marvell)

Swaying through loftier air,
Their new stratosphere—
Aggressive as palm trees,
Topknots nodding in a storm—
They gump towards us.

The bell, Round One, sounds
In their schoolyard hinterland.
Spring growth caught them unaware
Just as they had become confident at being kids,
Just as they'd worked out how to do it.

Now fine curls appear around clefts,
Legbones stretch on the rack,
Corrosive bases coursing through their blood
Cause stoops, bulging
Night-hurts and twitches.

A different face every morning.
Their bodies are betraying them
With chemicals. Organs flooded,
Gone tropical
With a bath of message toxins.

Adolescent boys slope towards adulthood
Forehead first and splayed spikes
Sutured across the brow-bone,
Eyeslits suspicious, puffed
And wounded by the future.

The seat of their soul has shifted
From stomach to testicles;
Blood now stings, lungs exhaust them
Games are no longer cub-cuffing,
But prize fights.

We are in the grace of age—
Hormonal acids long neutralised,
Thinned autumn-clear and painless—
And we can barely look at them
Tottering on narrowing centres of gravity.

We pass these morphing Quasimodos—
Excruciating as new knowledge—
As they lump along, raw,
Tough, inward wincing,
Bruised with youth.

Weathering their own rush of vegetable alkalis
The girls lean against the cyclone in clusters.
They are the same age as the boys
But much smarter: clever enough
To look worried.

Very worried.

A MAN OF RELIGION ATTENDS HIS FIRST AFL MATCH

I often visit the Junior School games,
Witness love and subsidy in parents' faces.
I arrange with Joel's mother to take him
For extra reading time this Monday.

Her husband has tickets to a game.
He and his friends kindly feed and water me.
Perhaps a little too gingerly;
It's the nature of the job, I'm afraid.

My expectations must have been foolishly high:
The sportsmen's muscular beauty, leaping heroism.
A small man shouts, "Farkin*shit*ouse! Sorry father."
Flustered, my only thought is to find his teacher.

Around me is spoken the tale of the game.
Harsh judgements of wayward bounces,
Of blindness, incompetent umpiring,
The evil and bastardry of all opponents.

Their passion scalds me. Events unfold,
But it doesn't seem to match what I hear.
Perhaps it is the story of their lives—
Pain and hungers irreconcilable.

The mascot sways, tugs its ropes—an idol
With teeth bared, perched on the oval's lip,
Strapped down like Gulliver,
Snarling a storybook curse.

Yellow runners are marginal glosses,
Transmitting messages to and from the zone.
Our team has won, it seems.
Snatched it. "Any win's a good win."

I thank Joel's dad, say I'll help his son
With his books again next week.
I leave the bitter crowd, poor in grace.
Love, too, may be a kind of absence.

A MAN'S POEM

That feeling, that thought
Sinks down into you,
sponging meaning
from around the lip
of the filter paper cone,
wiping its seashell gape,
an open spiral at the head—
hermit crab mandibles scissoring
tasting the fluid air;
then through the self,
flushed by body organs:
intensifying through the dense heart,
the lungs and lumpen torso,
that dark place below the ribs
where men tamp down
superfluous emotion;
the heavy, crammed gut, the bladder.
The molecules of residue—
sediment crystallising
magnified out of suspension—
in thick viscous anger
jostle furiously, shoving
with their spiny electrons.
And on the other side
its clear tincture
the pure poem
drips clear.

OUR FIELD OF DREAMS

Pressed against a bare wall
worlds come and go, blur and spin
through a clatter of motes and mortar
and off the rough frame into dark.
Colourised in Super 8, the picture
swings up from grass stubble,
across bessa-block clubrooms,
to Saturday arvo sportsmen
slugging it out for love.
Near the boundary, our brickie—
raw, artesian, blue collar,
pre-corporate—tugs his goatee,
waves off a picture hook, a fly,
hands up, armpit tussocks,
pulls a mark from the air,
hugs to kill, hails onlookers,
jabs at the lens, kicks on.

AGRARIAN GRIEVANCES

struck into couplets
by the rhythmic progression
of the hay wagon:

a revolutionary
economic paradigm

THE ANGEL AND THE FIG

She reaches, in the frozen attitude of flight—
But is on earth-duty. Souls in her care
Are protected, and saluted—venerated
By the woman from the Circle of cherubim.
But this angel is more than a sentry;
Set in bronze cast, she is trapped here.

Perhaps she picked fruit in her time on earth—
Her heavy forearms attest to such labour—
But this incarcerated spirit yearns towards
The great old fig tree, adjacent, unattainable,
Whose roots—an ornate plinth for limbs
Bearing its fat leaves and bitter fruit—paddle
And snake into this city's parochial earth and generations.

She gestures toward magic deeper than her own.
If she can touch it she will return to her proper place by god.

Some passing souls, encased in their own living bodies—
Those whose tender nerve-ends are exposed by love—
Are sensitive to the magnetism between the two poles
Of bronze and ionised trunk. They make the link for her.

She will grant lovers' wishes, give heart to sceptics,
If they will just cross the field hand in hand,
Close the circuit with their caresses, and connect her
Through desire and prayers and intimate thoughts
To the certainty that one day she will regain heaven.

JUNE CITY

across the prow of winter

a Greenpeace dinghy
braving the spume
of an oil tanker

leaves foam
and spray

about our ankles
as we dare this weather
to break us up and dump us

FINE CUT

a broad mat of smooth, glabrous fibre,
silken plush, sky-thin, earth red,
a fine undulating counterpane,
slow-rolling, wind-curled,
wraps your whole vision
horizon to deep horizon
over the membrane of the ocean,
over the skin of the sinuous air

a line slices straight
across the fabric's lustre
and the lips of the incision
separate, waving open;
a galaxy void
peers through the fissure,
molten, beckoning

this slash-rent, oil-ribbed landscape
teases your tingling nerve-tips,
skin raw from being cut out from the air,
it begs, whispering—
fold yourself in me
disappear in me, I am
where your senses end and the world begins
I bandage the wound of your body
let me envelop you
I will hold you

SET TOIL

Hollow

We fare pretty well, us men;
We aren't difficult, complex, like women.
Leave us alone together,
Head to head all we want to do is outclass
Our mates and rivals—good, clean fun. When
We get together
Are we going to care less—
As women do—about clean brass
Or income, or class,
In the pub at the bar?

Waste

Apes are what they are. Only care about breeding,
Lie when it suits them, rarely even good at fixing
Mementos they've knocked over and smashed, slurring
Dull-wittedly they're sorry. No brain.
Winter leaks in the house again, sandpit needs covering,
Earthworms in the compost want feeding.
A little holiday, no men or kids, is what I wish. Cuba's
Summer is glorious, I hear: I picture myself down at
    the sea
With a piña colada by my deckchair—or whisky
    and lemonade—
And a book, or massage; no kids vomiting and
    husband farting
And dogs shitting. Instead, warm sun, solitude. . . if only
    for an hour.

Assay

Because he smokes dope and burns the divan
Because he smokes dope
Because he smokes dope and burns
Desiring to watch The Footy Show, then hope
I will be in the mood for a bit of tubering
("Why not?" he grunts. "Better than arguing.")
Why shouldn't I mourn
The vanished love and wonder why I've remained?

Proof

Let go. It's the end for you and I.
When you do nothing but talk about her, praise her to
    the sky,
Like I don't get what's going on. Well, here are *my* cards on
    the table:
Let go. Don't you think when I and my friends hit
    the streets,
The cafés, that we don't pick up occasional treats?
Of those, well, one or two have persuaded me to hotels
And country retreats. Shocked? You've dropped your
    own bombshells:
Streets I've glimpsed you in; that love document
Of hers—pornographic in content.
To leave her underwear under the bed begs the question. . .
Oh, do not ask "What is it?"
Let's just accept that This is *it*.

CUPID'S DAY

Aspiring high was Cupid, son of Venus, carrying aloft
With him a quiverful of golden arrows which had oft
Aforetimes piercèd mortal hearts inflicting wounds therein
That caused the strongest wills or oaths to turn and
    fresh begin
In seeking love: a bootless target or a happy goal,
That burieth men in damnèd plots, or succoureth their souls.

Now Cupid, mounting to the airy spheres that gleam above,
Purposed to knit all souls on troubled earth in
    prosperous love
By piercing both the moon and fiery sun with golden darts
And so reflecting night and day the influence of the heart.
Unblindfolded, then, he flew, ascending straight apeak
Towards the heavens and the orbs celestial he did seek.

He travelled 'twixt the dark and light in cloudy
    regions grey—
The borderline where ne day-sun nor moonlit night
    held sway,
Where neither it was dusk nor dawn, and both the
    glowing spheres
Contended, one to heat, the other cool, and therefore here
The clime was temperate—so Cupid could approach close by
And aim his shafts with surety: the which he did let fly.

Swift-winged sped a golden arrow to the flaming sun,
But melted straight and fell to earth as gold among the dun.
And where it fell sprang yellow blooms from which if ta'en
    the juice
And mixt in drink inflicteth love on whomsoever ye choose.

The dart that pierced white Phoebe could no
    penetration make
And fell back bringing Lunar rocks and loose earth in
    its wake
That charmèd by the shaft from Cupid's bow became the soil
Upon which mortal creatures tread and love, baseborn
    or royal.

Cupid, then, whose self-made task had failed, brooked
    no delay
In presently returning, yet fore'er to mark the day
As one when not all souls had been infusèd with high love
But let fall from the heavens sweet aspersions like the dove
Which with its downy wings doth, oft unlook'd for, touch
    with joy
Those fortunate folk who with prayers bless Venus'
    young envoy.

POET REMEETS MUSE

It was too rich, too perfumed;
Air thickened, and congealed in his lungs.

He knew he must retreat to familiar heights
Where the atmosphere was austere, sharp in his sinus.

The touch of a warm hand was enough
To set pen in motion;

But a shoulder, throat, hair,
Was like swimming through honey.

Best to await a still moment on a family holiday,
The hypnosis of domestic pleasures;

Best to invoke her amongst the safety of
Waves on steady cliffs, orderly clouds,

The even clarity of squaring away the lawn;
Stay pure and preserved in rarefied amber light,

And tease his writing towards a semblance of passion,
    using her
To oxygenate his poems.

PROFESSIONAL LOVE

The Commissioner gave me a hug.
I make her lips move onstage, I accompany her,
But where had she been the last two weeks?
"Welcome back!" Return hug. Kobe conference?
Beijing Congress? Should I have known it?

The Attorney General shook my hand.
"Hello again, Stephen." He read my name tag;
Working the room. "Hello, Robert." (Too familiar.)
His speechwriter looked at me askance, blinked.
I blinked back. He thought: I'm a lawyer, you're not.

The Minister glanced my way, pointed
Like a Thai dancer, tapped his glasses. A job offer?
He had heard my piece at that breakfast Forum.
Clever but conservative. Witty but safe. Most apt.
I'll call his assistant, about a joint project, something.

The Premier sat down in my chair.
I had moved aside—away from my CEO—
For just such a contingency: allow her to sit by him;
An opportunity for the pair to talk about that Bill
Amending our legislation. But fuck him anyway.

The Commissioner hugged me, again, yesterday.
"It's Singapore's pre-Monsoon. Your family will love it."
I will devote myself to her and advance her any way
    I can.
The Commissioner gave me a hug. She loves me.
I love her. And she is my chosen profession.

HOW NOT TO KILL
GOVERNMENT LEADERS

Whenever I'm with the Prime Minister
I want to assassinate him.
Not just pat his shiny head for the media,
say "Stuffed up. Bad job"—but pull a gun
Bang-Bang. Bang.

We all do. A tic, a scrotal itch implanted
by childhood news reports:
Our generation has lived all its life
with this footage. Foggy blasts of chaos
roost in our minds.

I pat my empty jacket; we stand inside
a magic circle of minders.
Although they know me by now,
they sense the compulsion I endure
and are confused.

Squeezed by a warm security scrum,
my trigger-finger snapped,
yanked numb—validating my syndrome,
and their existence, with dim, binding
pressure, steel restraint.

But he flatters me: "Admirable launch."
My neurosis detumesces.
Meaningless CEO flirtation swamps
pricking symptoms, killer brain cells,
with its special drug.

He weakly wrings my weaponless hand.
Eyes drift to the next morsel.
The bright circle browses to another constituent.
I scratch myself. The Prime Minister is safe.
Bastard.

POLITICAL DEBATE

mayflies' secret love-dance
lunge, hold the other immobile
like dog and hare in a death-grip
locked onto key organs, frozen
in their dignified, guttural intimacy

ACTS

The Children and Young Persons (Care and Protection) Act
    1998—hereinafter "the Act"—was . . .
Passed? No, not passed not quite passed, but.
The Children and Young Persons (Care and Protection) Act
    1998—hereinafter "the Act"—was—
Not passed, but—*assented* to.
Assented to by the NSW Parliament in December 1998.
Yes, it was assented to. The Act was assented to
    in December.
But this was after much consultation.
Much consultation. Extensive consultation.
After an extensive consultative process over a three-
    year period.
Yes, and a review. A review.
An extensive, three-year consultative process and a review.
A review of what? Of what?
Of the Children (Care and Protection) Act 1987 (NSW)—
    hereinafter "the 1987 Act."
A review of the Children (Care and Protection) Act 1987
    (NSW)—hereinafter "the 1987 Act."
A review of the 1987 Act.
The 1987 Act, that was, up to that time, the most extensive,
    the most extensive review of the legislation.
Many. Many of the initiatives were widely widely discussed.
Discussed by working parties and welcomed by the sector.
The names of agencies?
The name or names of agencies consulted? Agencies and
    providers consulted as a part of the review?
The organisations and providers and agencies that were
    consulted—that have been—that were consulted.
The names. Are. Include.

The Legal Aid Commission, the NSW Anti-Discrimination
Board, the Australian Commercial Dispute Centre,
Relationships Australia and the Community
Justice . . . network—
Hereinafter, the LAC ADB ACDC RA CJC . . . network.
Interagency working groups amongst these networks.
Working parties. Examined the application of these matters
and made recommendations.
Recommendations? Recommendations for?
For Service Models. For use within the sector.
It is an initiative. A significant initiative—a cross-
jurisdictional, an interagency, initiative.
Including enacted models from organisations—from
agencies—such as the LAC ADB ACDC RA CJC
. . . network.
Yes. A paper is available.
For those with more questions, a discussion paper is available.
A paper that discusses and documents the likely moves to
progress the implementation.
Yes. The discussion paper can be found. It can be sourced at
www.community.nsw.gov[gee-oh-vee].au.
This is not to be confused with the Review chairperson's
Review Report of the 1987 Act.
The recommendations of the Review Report of the 1987 Act
can be sourced can also be sourced at
www.community.nsw.gov.au.
Implementation is pending.
Implementation of the recommendations is pending.
Until solutions.
Until workable solutions optimal solutions are in place.
Until workable solutions are found and set in place—
Concerning the actions that need to take place as a result of
the discussion paper that arose from working parties
carrying out extensive interagency consultation—

Implementation is pending.
The discussion paper is available, to illustrate the likely
    progress of the recommendations—
But until then . . .
Implementation is pending.

MEETING WITH THE COUNTY BOARD OF EDUCATION TO GLEAN SUPPORT TO APPROACH THE LOCAL COUNCIL FOR BACKING

In an effort to prepare for the meeting.
In an effort to prepare for the meeting,
I constructed a seven-element chart,
For myself as well as for the Board.
In order to focus my thoughts,
I constructed a seven-element chart.
The seven-element chart.
The seven-element analysis.
The seven-element analysis is a diagnostic tool.
The seven-element tool
Is not to be confused with
The four-quadrant analysis
Which is a diagnostic tool
To take a view of a situation from a macro level,
From a *macro* perspective.
The seven-element chart is another diagnostic tool.
The seven-element tool
Provides a more detailed, *micro* analysis.
A micro analysis of the presenting situation.
In order to systematically prepare for the meeting
I constructed a chart.
The chart allowed me to focus
On what I really wanted to achieve
Out of the meeting.
The chart—the seven-element chart—
Allowed me to identify outcomes,
Good outcomes, the numerous possible outcomes.
The chart—the tool—clarified the outcomes,
In a systematic way; clarified—
Clarified and allowed me to focus on—

What I really wanted to achieve at this meeting.
The seven-element tool gave me a yardstick
To evaluate the possible outcomes,
To realistically evaluate and diagnose
The possible options.
The tool's objective standard allowed me
To benchmark the possible options on the table.
I constructed the seven-element chart
In an effort to prepare for the meeting,
In an effort to prepare for the meeting
I have laid the groundwork for a resolution,
A resolution to be passed by the Board,
For an in-principle substantive agreement,
An in-principle commitment—
An agreement, a process commitment
In the form of a timetable,
To finalise out the details.
A timetable for consultation, research
And future meetings;
To finalise out the details
Of how such a program,
How such a schedule would work —
And to finalise out the details
Of future meetings.

LOGICAL ARGUMENT

declamatory
flying buttresses, a
rococo volute,

the sarcastic rejoinder,
with rhetorical flourish

CATSCAN

brain in a ham slice, pushed
scalp-first, blood-luminous
into the spinning Stargate—
an aero-fibreglass Time Tunnel—
reading my cerebral IQ
blood clot by blood clot

DEMENTIA

the world pixellates
fine perceptions replaced
by grosser information
binary digits, block-sized
complex processing
degraded, rerouted
down narrow side-alleys
too deficient in bps
for brimming lorryloads
pushing through their burden

WATER AND AIR

The slender glass twister dances,
neurotic, teasing and toeing, passing over
each segment of the drain-grate,
hair-fine, agitated, never settling on one cell or another,
flirting with the void
that pulls matter through its foursquare lattice;

the molten vase unknots itself downwards,
turning, hopping and tapping, furious now,
twisting, haughtily snorting—
seeking to wriggle away from the inevitable
with its electric tip, fragile and enraged,
gulping, choking, betrayed;

water's artefact, abandoned by matter's parting,
fattens to a thunderous slurp,
gasps, trickles, rattles and clunks apart; now it
opens out into the atmosphere, fills the quieting
    emptiness,
and becomes the air that is all things.
It is nothing.

SWAN RISES

black swan clatters up
trying to lever itself
into the clear air;
struggles, hooks it neck ahead
labouring through nothingness

HAZARDOUS ACCUMULATIONS

1.
The tray clamps cash: it's
a liquidity event
at my ATM.

2.
Too poor to invest?
Adjust your acquisition
benchmark way downwards.

3.
Twenty? No. No deal.
Even ten is excessive.
So—ten then? Okay.

4.
High-end prostitute
wants an exit strategy?
Try studying law.

5.
Then my mobile rings—
throbbing, black, the size of a
Sydney cockroach.

6.
Mobile text message:
CALL ME NOW FOR A GREAT DEAL
(conditions apply).

7.
Satellite broadcast:
like a Star Trek tricorder
my pager alerts me.

8.
Note: Due to problems,
sending and receiving mail
is impossible.

9.
A watch so complex
I have to hack into it
to find out the time.

10.
Zero nine hundred.
Do not activate weapons:
I'll give the signal.

11.
This is the machine.
I am the ghost. Please speak now.
You are the message.

12.
Try this word. Here goes. . .
it's: TRANSUBSTANTIATION
ALISTICALLY.

13.
I am so stingy
when I steal I only take
things I can afford.

14.
This line of haiku—
squelched, squelched, squelched, squelched, squelched,
      squelched, squelched—
is my longest plod.

15.
i heard these poems
and laughed uproariously
then i fell over

16.
Seventeen, sixteen,
sixteen, seventeen, sixteen,
seventeen, sixteen.

17.
Seventeen, sixteen,
fifteen, fourteen, thirteen-. . .
three, two, one, zero.

18.
One, two, three, four, five
senses working overtime;
truth bells softly chime.

18.
Every time we doubt,
god intervenes and tells us:
Two plus two is five.

19.
Two children's war books:
'Toby and the Tet Offensive',
'Holocaust Hazel'.

20.
Emotions stop you
from seeing that they are all
that is important.

21.
fresh-creeping about
the tastes and smells and odours
of Spring, as they thaw

22.
Bees swarm my daughter;
they tell her she's a woman
before she knows herself.

23.
Bad, good—which to be?
O, let a lady confess:
I want to be bad.

24.
A schoolboy is caught
with a lass dressed as a lad
in the prefect's room.

25.
Priest in confessional:
"You did *what*! That makes me mad.
Get out of this box."

26.
Are you kidding me?
I'll pretend I didn't hear—
and I won't reply.

27.
My church privatised
meditation: outsourced to
the business sector.

28.
After I left school
they called it dyslexia.
But I was just dumb.

29.
I was the subject,
in a twelve-year study, who
got the placebo.

30.
I once suffered from
Attention Deficit Dis. . .
Look at that great view.

31.
Eighteenth century
expansionist seafaring:
"Colonise", "Terrain".

32.
Well-travelled enough
well-educated enough
to be unhappy.

33.
Small, muscled beasts glimpsed
(naturally-occurring
steroids) in the bush.

34.
The Free Olympics
in 2012 will outlaw
drug tests for athletes.

35.
National Anthem:
"Ozzie. Ozzie. Ozzie. Oi.
Oi. Oi." Know the words?

36.
Fingers meander
their spastic way crutchward, on
invisible frets.

37.
— . . . just heard J.S. Bach's
Biddleyouvee 564,
Toccata in C.

38.
Karajan conducts
like he's a washerwoman
doing the scrubbing.

39.
Strings gushed out, as from
a broad, flat fissure in a
rusted water-tank.

40.
something poisonous
folded in layers of cloth
glows amongst the clouds

41.
shafts stalk the ocean—
sun broken through clouds' ceiling—
slow, massive searchlights

42.
I'm not a hero—
not any kind of hero—
a wall fell on me.

43.
A mole burrows through
the back of a skull. It thinks
it's still underground.

44.
When worries stay mute,
when dishonesty creeps in,
the friendship's matured.

45.
It's Friday, and drinks
are imminent at the pub.
So this means . . . I'm gone.

46.
I'm close enough to
my friends to be perfectly
alienated.

47.
A row of portraits
sends the lonely browser
past each stern gaze.

48.
With a cigarette
near his ear, he sits alone
communing with it.

49.
My wife lost a child
years ago; there's still a ghost
in the family.

50.
By their mid forties
life has commonly driven
most people insane.

51.
You hate me. So leave.
I'm diminished, small, selfish,
foolish in your eyes.

52.
peering back at earth
through the cast-off, burnt-out ring
of my second stage

53.
My wrong turn offers
a postcoital taking-stock,
a fresh, focused start.

54.
I'm past the point where
I can respectably stage
a midlife crisis.

55.
watercolour sky,
cerise clouds, cause hazardous
accumulations

56.
a jutting outcrop
of slate pierces the clouded
membrane of vision

57.
water tower looms
derelict—a condiment
among city streets

58.
sky pours down
softens the outline to a
ruined silhouette

59.
grey sparrows twitter
sewing themselves in to roost—
treetop tapestries

60.
The paste of their dead—
ants crushed by human toes—tastes
sickly, like sweetmeat.

61.
Wheelchairs are boys' toys;
rendered immobile, women
would rather stay put.

62.
I respect the church,
and grieve, for the human thought
that's gone into it.

63.
Rags against the cold,
worn books warm me—while the young
rage against the old.

64.
Heartbeat monitor:
the old car's indicator
clicked, stuttered and blinked.

65.
Age chooses for you;
age is how you see the world;
age is all you are.

66.
Age chose it for you;
age was how you saw the world;
age is all you are.

THE
AMMONITE
STAIRWELL

("eating the toilet bowl in the gingerbread house")

FIFTEEN KINDS OF FOOTNOTE

The text persuades, the note proves
(The Footnote—Anthony Grafton)

1. Factoid
Sperm, unfrozen, through momentary windows glimpse
     light,
Tail-kick into the reader's view.
Made it! Makes it from archive-sac into scholar's
     notebook;
Stirs around excitedly. The Book! Then
The next great push—jostling with a cluster of
     companioncompetitors—
Survives intact into the footnote.
The footnote! Passes its genetic code into the book's
     organic argument.
Cells divide and differentiate;
If all goes well, very well—a foetus delivers itself to
     the world:
The Book Review!

2. Turnoff
Crosstown artery. Eighty-nine. Rain. Third lane in.
An aqueduct—linear, planar—through a forest of
     highrise ideas.

Forced turn at the sign of a cross, green-smeared
     overhead—
Brake, answering brain-stem training. Sodden traffic
     howls.

The church—small town stone-by-stone building history
     by the font,
One wall a flying freeway buttress—offers little solace at
     rush hour.

No feeder back. Gap in a service road. Pull into
    merciless traffic,
Tyres crackle spray. Zero to ninety; forced to regain
    momentum in an eyeblink.
Window wipes into a widow's peak. Another tourist sign.
One-eleven. Don't think about it. I turn my eyes from
    god. Race on.

3. Cf.
The conferral, the comparison,
The scholarly sneer.
Discutable. Injects black die into the reference,
Turns a footnote into its negative.

It is acknowledged, it is indulged . . .
It is wrong.
Ganz abwegig. The Judas kiss,
Embrace slyly then cast to the dogs.

Indispensable academic apparatus.

4. Typography
The ring, at whose stone flush we cannot closely focus,
Seems to drop our eyes into Aladdin's cave.

Laquear side-chapel. The cardinal's vestments;
The outward and visible sign of inward grace

Adopted when religion corporatised—
And when eloquent narrative became critical discipline.

The marriage of history and philology,
Making their child legitimate.

5. Scriptural Commentaries
This huge bible-bomb:
Rough handling by ordinary persons—
Colloquial usage by the common herd,
Those unskilled in doctrine,
The proletariat—might set it off.

This giant onion:
Vulgate edition, St. Jerome;
Shakespeare's English; Bishop's text;
Peel to Latin; deeper, Greek, Hebrew;
An empty core revealing a death's head.

This immense globe:
Translations are the explosives experts
Returning with complex, dirty grins,
Latex glove stamped with church's sanction,
Displaying their cut wires like tablets.

This great bulb:
Notes scurry, mere sycophants, eunuch acolytes,
Intermediaries between the divine words
And the lay reader, the coarse public,
Dimly aware of their need for prostration, oblivion.

6. Disposal
Cesspool city. Text droppings.
Open sewers, sluggish;
entropy's leavings puddled
within a shallow scoop
of tight paving and walkways.

The factory's waste,
tagged and buried drums
(a faint night-glow),
at highly publicised locations
in shoaled graves.

7. Weald

Hidden within the forest, little people,
mischievous, teasing us at vision's periphery.
We crane towards the canopy; a tree frog
secured to the smooth trunk with sucker pads.
Tracking back from the high green—leaves
livid, artful, sunsoaked—to root systems
ranging through bleak, acidic subsoil.
Our retina catches on a movement; we turn,
focus our pattern-seeking machinery.
We trip over a root. Small voices taunt.

8. Archival Professionalism

business cards
scattered
cheese flags
denoting
hard work

9. Citation

Historians cite authorities
Lawyers cite sources.

Historians cite collateral evidence
Journalists cite a principal source.

Historians' conclusions are corrected
Theologians' conclusions are supplemented.

10. Critical Scrutiny

Terrain damaged by artillery hidden
impregnable behind a bunker of low, mud-ivory hills

(for the news shot
a war correspondent coaxes his tripod's ankles)—

footsoldiers in the tank's wake
are picked off, fall open, crouch into their entrails

hair, skin, nails blown by a barrage
of tiny, invisible gusts, crumbling them to pulp—

but, methodical, with irresistible purpose,
an entreaty of metal plate borne upon lockstep iron
    treads,

convinces the clay landscape,
this discourse of blasted territory, to yield a few metres.

11. Hiatus in MS
****
****

****
****

****
****

****
****

12. Epigoni
J'appartiens à une génération qui n'est plus jeune.

Once, the writer did the work, scattered references
Like gentle seasoning, inviting the reader to verify.

My son clumps into our workshop home for supper;
His boots engulf his lean ankles, like a club-foot.

Once, elegance, self-effacement was a duty;
But learning has changed its form and method.

My stew is perfect, tasty, vegetable and meat;
But he takes the shaker—salts, and salts some more.

Nowadays, paraphernalia, *l'appareil d'érudition*,
The show and fashion of formality, burdens our craft.

He kicks my delicate carven teak as he sits, then
Parades off, stomping, disfigured by his swollen feet.

I have passed my riches on to my son.
I belong to a generation no longer young.

13. The Variorum Shakespeare
barely glimpsing its reflection—
a hazy dot against algal murk—

the glow-worm flits and shivers,
a wisp, over clutching swamps

14. The Fruit of the Tree of Source-Criticism
hung on branch-tips
of one dendritic form amongst shrubs and walkways

threading roots upwards,
veins feeding from the swollen, silhouette sky.

The stylist took a bite
and became an academic historian.

Cast out, the historian,
unable now to compose a simple narrative,

took to tilling dry soil,
turning up chunks of shale and granite with his tools;

mica-glittering walls,
constructed to herd beasts and corral his crops.

15. Endnote
Practical exposition.

The gloss.
The scholium.
The caption.
The adversaria.
Exegetics.
Hermeneutics.

To render.
To construe.
Paraphrast.
Palaeography.

The asterix.
The crucifix.
The footnote.
The numeral.
Arabic.
Greek and Roman.

Apparatus criticus.

Supertext.

POETRY

~~the act~~ ~~of creation~~
~~of creation~~
poetry ~~has, like life,~~
is ~~order in chaos~~
~~arising~~
~~growing out of laws~~ ~~built upon~~
~~built upon the contours of living~~
~~rules and structures~~
~~surrounding us~~ like ~~a womb~~
~~like~~ what we do during the day

IAMBS

silently counting
the poet opens his fist
finger by finger

holding his hand poised
fingertips ripple and nod,
a shadow puppet

spider jerks its legs
wary at the first whiff
of insecticide

IS THIS POETRY?

1.
Is this poetry?
Eating the toilet bowl in
the gingerbread house.

2.
Is this poetry?
There will be no performance
without a license.

3.
Is this poetry?
Our story begins. And ends.
Very violently.

4.
Is this poetry?
Sleep, fitness, work, family
are impediments.

5.
Is this poetry?
No, it's a brain blender—not
a coffee filter.

6.
Is this poetry?
Song to my dying mother:
'K-K-K-Katy . . .'

7.
Is this poetry?
Songs to which guard droids listen
at their down-time clubs.

8.
Is this poetry?
On your knees! Pray to the Muse.
Go on. Do it. Now!

9.
Is this poetry?
You pull the head off the doll?
You don't want the doll.

10.
Is this poetry?
'Prosody and Poesy'
by Patty Pipkin.

11.
Is this poetry?
'Vivien Vineland's Vocal
Versified Vignettes.'

12.
Is this poetry?
'Ophelia Opaline's
Obscene Oral Odes.'

13.
Is this poetry?
"I love you." If you say it,
then you must mean it.

14.
Is this poetry?
Don't unplan. Create the plan.
Then transcend the plan.

15.
Is this poetry?
My kids are younger, smaller,
and they're less mature.

16.
Is this poetry?
I don't distribute leaflets;
they are Proposals.

17.
Is this poetry?
I watch as other people
bounce on trampolines.

18.
Is this poetry?
Nothing is more dangerous
than well-refined wit.

19.
Is this poetry?
A keyboard's tiny clatter:
a pixie's car starts.

20.
Is this poetry?
I drop the black chess pieces
down a flight of stairs.

21.
Is this poetry?
The occupation's hazard
is intimacy.

22.
Is this poetry?
Wrapping one's seriousness
round such tiny things.

23.
Is this poetry?
If a smart person loves you,
they know you wholly.

24.
Is this poetry?
I don't want to know people—
just understand them.

25.
Is this poetry?
If society could think
it would fall apart.

26.
Is this poetry?
Sidelong, colons are blank eyes,
brackets smiles or frowns.

27.
is this poetry
unfettered verse compromised
the Honorific

28.
(Is: this, poetry?)
Words—jargon—as 'hard' design;
readable-graphics.

29.
Is this poetry?
My keystrokes poeticise
corporate reports.

30.
Is this poetry?
A relentless electro-
chemical sheep-dip.

31.
Is this poetry?
The growing heart of blast-heat
bursts through the steel shell.

32.
Is this poetry?
Sandcastle-building contests
at the festival.

33.
Is this poetry?
Wind is language, a soft force
that bends the swan's path.

34.
Is this poetry?
Father's last wish: Keep me in
the conversation.

35.
Is this poetry?
The sandal's stenography:
foot calligraphy.

36.
Is this poetry?
A politician's sound-bite
is a prose haiku.

37.
Is this poetry?
A big bell, symbolising
the town's industry.

38.
Is this poetry?
The first-built megabillboards
in Communist towns.

39.
Is this poetry?
He who gives himself to death
is hardest to kill.

40.
Is this poetry?
The penis, the pen, withdraws
wet as spaghetti.

41.
Is this poetry?
He's not gay—but he's a queen.
You know what I mean.

42.
Is this poetry?
Old age stained with deism—
yellowed fingertips.

43.
Is this poetry?
Peering through ammonite curls:
stone spiral stairwell.

44.
Is this poetry?
I view the plane fall, inflight—
gape down its aisle's tilt.

45.
Is this poetry?
A snakehead's brief rippled wake:
fingers smear the screen.

46.
Is this poetry?
* * white * * * *
* syntax * *

47.
Is this poetry?
Laughter through a thick membrane
emerges heartfelt.

48.
Is this poetry?
A cricket chirrs through the night,
braids dark together.

49.
Is this poetry?
Parliament House, Canberra:
bunched typewriter keys.

50.
Is this poetry?
Azaria Chamberlain's
21st birthday.

51.
Is this poetry?
I compose like I'm having
an asthma attack.

52.
Is this poetry?
From a balcony I stroke
my pet, the city.

53.
Is this poetry?
Islands' negatives, strayed lakes
have got lost inland.

54.
Is this poetry?
Writing's most embarrassing
and poorest cousin.

55.
Is this poetry?
As spacious as the Tardis:
folders in Windows.

56.
Is this poetry?
Thoughts supported by head-dips
of angry pigeons.

57.
Is this poetry?
My sinuses click and tweet;
bats flit between trees.

58.
Is this poetry?
Stupid. No, wait. Correction:
Damn bloody stupid.

59.
Is this poetry?
Writers see less of the world
as they grow older.

60.
Is this poetry?
We heave art into the air,
tossing a caber.

61.
Is this poetry?
To remove excess lipstick,
press lips to tissue.

62.
Is this poetry?
Always listen more closely
to those you despise.

63.
Is this poetry?
Short poems must justify
their art more strongly.

64.
Is this poetry?
An artwork argues for its
own reality.

65.
Is this poetry?
Soaked up by ambient noise,
a distant signal.

66.
Is this poetry?
Radio music heard faint,
damaged and ragged.

67.
Is this poetry?
Hourly news buttons the day—
small, polished, dense nodes.

68.
Is this poetry?
Crazy cirrus whips cloud-cattle
to the distant hills.

69.
Is this poetry?
Critics pin superlatives
on Art, like brooches.

70.
Is this poetry?
The fashion superhighway—
and we are roadkill.

71.
Is this poetry?
Hiding within the circle
of my daughter's face.

72.
Is this poetry?
Sal. Sally. Silly. Dibbie.
Dabbie. Debbie. Deb.

73.
Is this poetry?
Racing to the next bargain,
autumn leaves panic.

74.
Is this poetry?
George & Martha's Blended Tea:
"AFTERNOON RESPITE".

75.
Is this poetry?
Poetic form is flotsam
in the rush to know.

76.
Is this poetry?
Who would dare say it wasn't?
It must be, right? Right?

77.
Is this poetry?
I don't want to read it, so
I reckon it is.

78.
Is this poetry?
Our half-educated guilt
sells poetry books.

79.
Is this poetry?
I am strongly-versed in the
oral tradition.

80.
Is this poetry?
Hughes provides obbligato
throughout all my works.

81.
"I'm impressed," you said—
insincerely, but impressed.
Is this poetry?

82.
Is this poetry?
No-one can now pretend they're
under the radar.

83.
Is this poetry?
Winter holds my wrists and cheek
tenderly, sweetly.

84.
Is this poetry?
Reconfigure the future
kicking at random.

85.
Is this poetry?
People don't pray in church, or
meditate; they brood.

86.
Is this poetry—
relevant as magnetic
strips—when that isn't?

87.
Is this poetry?
My Imaginary Friends:
unwritten poems.

88.
Is this poetry?
Holding party caviar
biscuits like tickets.

89.
Is this poetry?
An artery's corpuscles
pulled back to the heart.

90.
 Is this poetry?
The present is the point of
time's dissolution.

91.
Is this poetry?
The dead think that the living
are ghosts of the dead.

92.
Is this poetry?
An atheist, I believe
in the Universe.*

94.
Is this poetry?
We go to the party dressed
as an emotion.

95.
Is this poetry?
Blind since I was twelve, I'm a
connoisseur of pain.

---

* 93.

— — — — —

You see your god in your way;
I'll see him in His.

96.
Is this poetry?
the wind's fibres are marked by
the water's surface

97.
Is this poetry?
Raucous intimacy of
oboe, clarinet.

98.
Is this poetry?
rain patters on the window—
harpsichord trickles

99.
Is this poetry?
My line through to the US
spits, scratches and fumes.

100.
Is this poetry?
Writer's face congeals around
the rim of her mouth.

101.
Is this poetry?
Have an orgasm laughing?
It's impossible.

102.
Is this poetry?
Music of the cooling earth
sings the death of light.

103.
Is this poetry?
In grotesque supplication
tree limbs reach to me.

104.
Is this poetry?
Tapping, his toes' callous-pads
chuff like a steamtrain.

105.
Is this poetry?
Her sobs sawed through the black air,
shark fins approaching.

106.
Is this poetry?
Dissolving upon itself,
the motorboat turns.

107.
Is this poetry?
Here I am, a dry old man
in a dry season.

108.
Is this poetry?
April is the cruellest month.
Datta. Damyata.

109.
Is this poetry?
The cathedral's spire thrusts from
its missile silo.

110.
Is this poetry?
Pinning down the sea's edges,
cocklers search the beach.

111.
Is this poetry?
Exploring sonorities
at the piano.

111.
Is this poetry?
My vulnerability
took years to perfect.

112.
Is this poetry?
Start writing a Mills & Boon;
end with parody.

113.
Is this poetry?
Behavioural Psychology
isn't what you think.

114.
Is this poetry?
What a choice a writer has
in one syllable!

115.
Is this poetry?
Do you fear dissolution
and death? Yes, and no.

116.
Is this poetry?
Who me? I'm not a poet.
How well I know it.

117.
Is this poetry?
Thou, the Onlie Begetter
of These Sonnets.

THE CAST

1.
The Cast: A Watchman,
A Ghost, Revenge, Halberdiers,
Devils and Spirits.

2.
The Cast: The Marquesse,
A Lady, afterwards Queen,
Divers Attendants.

3.
The Cast: Two Children,
Queen of the Goths, Officers,
Emperor of Rome.

4.
The Cast: General
of the French Forces, la Pucelle,
Their Son, Murderers.

5.
The Cast: An Old Man,
A Scythian Shepherdess,
The Prince of Egypt.

6.
The Cast: The right Duke,
His Page, The usurping Duke
and His Followers.

7.
The cast: Jupiter,
Juno, Hermes, Ganymede,
Cupid, Venus, Doves.

8.
The Cast: Turtledoves,
A Partridge in a Pear Tree,
Lady's Shoe, Lord's Boot.

9.
The Cast: Shrinking Parts,
One exhausted Director,
Prowling Producers.

10.
The Cast: Pope of Rome,
A Bawd, A Thief, A Dancer,
Other Retainers.

11.
The Cast: Archbishop
of Canterbury, Hostess
of Eastcheap Tavern.

12.
The Cast: Two Ladies,
A fantastical Spaniard,
A French Physician.

13.
The Cast: Twelve Trumpets,
Sackbuts, Hautbois, Alpine Horns,
A Bellows-mender.

14.
The Cast: Shipmaster,
Mariners, A young Boatswain,
A disguised Princess.

15.
The Cast: Two Outlaws,
Foresters, A rustic Wench,
A Country Justice.

16.
The Cast: The Old Queen,
An amarous Groom, his Boy,
Apothecary.

17.
The Cast: Ryche Folkes,
Pursuivants to Heralds,
Twenty Creditors.

18.
The Cast: Presenter,
Reader of the Epilogue,
Lights, Sound, Director.

NATIONAL GALLERY OF MODERN ART

splayed worms of
toothpaste greenyellow

meathooks and
smashed glass

drip-dry
pollockvomit

twisted truths of
the photoreal

radio-static abstracts
sculpt your awareness

black molten
rock erotica

coffee and cakes
from our modern cafe

STATE GALLERY OF MODERN ART

grubs of green-red sport
upon sprayed starscapes

chemical-damp Kodaks
scarred and knifesmeared

a silent black wall
expounds Theory's mystery

laser-lit bytes
dancing electron-coloured

shredded canvas flags proclaim
I AM

ox-heart teased apart
with fishhooks and ribbon

coffee and cakes
from our modern cafe

TANGLED IN THE HANGING SCULPTURE

a genetic disease
in a DNA spiral
of suspended
ping pong balls

THE LIP
ABACUS

("ankle-deep in the Santos-blue river, unreeling")

AUSTRALIANS AT PEACE

"The King's Writ runs, the King's peace observed.
"The Crown is our nexus." (The Empire
Parliamentary Association thanks Mr Menzies
For his colonial enthusiasm.) The war cools.
Just off the boil, in 1948. A mid century morning
Comes across the sky. The world is close around.

Hotpoint. Wundawax Floor Polish. Johnson & Johnson.
Household names. Local factories and multinationals—
New emblems, positioning themselves in the economy—
Tumble in market bags, throng and jostle in the pantry.
Velvet Soap for fabrics. Bon Ami for kitchens.
Kix Fly spray containing DDT the wonder chemical,
Dusts our gardens, pumps into our domestic spaces
By pleated mums, bleached, even-toothed, radiant.
A team of researchers (two are American—buddies
Taking turns at night to wire home data and results);
Down at the Ag Department—rosemary and lilly pilly
Shoulder through the rubbled landscape around
Fresh foursquare government buildings, eucalypts
Dust the sky further off—they pore over glass cages
At mutant roaches scuffling over their dying parents.

Surgeons open the heart-muscle, repair it; the patient
On his slab, briefly reprieved, awakens, hears the
    Olympics
Commence through his hospital window, then dies.
Princess Elizabeth—wedding presents not yet arranged
For display or placed in safekeeping or responded to
With diplomatic gratitude to powers stable and rising—
Has grown out of fine gowns, gathered dresses.
In her belly, Charles' line is dimmed, displaced
By wartime Allies. Bradman's Invincibles tour England.

The War confirmed borders, established others;
It is up to labour and capital to protect them.
The UN. The US. Countries rush to marshal the future.
Co-operatives rebuild industry in India, Europe, China.
Japan in Occupation—spread pinned, samurai-
    impassive—
Allows tourists to tickle its folds, enter its markets,
Prick and sting modern commerce into being.
"Konnichi wa. Wristwatch? Jacket?" "No, no.
Where. Is. The sea. Port?" "Iie. Watashi wa
Wakarimasen. Hiro san. Wakarimasuka?"
"Sukoshi. Yes. A rittle bit." "I. Am. Australian."
"Oh. Hai, hai. Anata no oökïi YANKEE desu."

Seeing their chance, other ancient countries
Shackled by ocean powers, by new kinds of death,
Indulge the postwar luxury of instability:
Independent Israel promptly wars with Arabs,
Indonesian nationalists battle Dutch colonials.
Gandhi falls (assassination is a peacetime activity).

Papua and New Guinea. An elder, and man-son
(Clothed, fresh from Moresby, ready to make money),
At Idler's Bay tearing strips from old Woman's Weekly.
Coppergreen palms, wind-bent, jostle and nod topknots.
Some pages they keep intact for big transactions:
Cattle, water pumps, land. The banker now holds
The tribe's currency. Shells are out of circulation.
In the water a child finger-shoots, dives akimbo
From a rusting mine, shrieks like a newborn potentate.

"*You're not in a prison camp now*"—Bonegilla.
Unloaded from trains, buses, the first 12,000 welcomed:
"*Australians and migrants are treated equally!*"
Black winter greatcoats clog camp bins—hides of extinct
European beasts. "*You'll learn the Australian way of life.*"
Magazine correspondents stroll the corrugated carapace
Of the barracks—lavender and rock rose seedlings

Displace stones dusted white and orange, popping
Like distant gunfire then crumbling underfoot—
Seeking copy from inmates with refugee English.
To sternly coquettish girls: "What pretty faces—
Are there camp romances? You were a gymnast?
In Hitler's Games? Will you care to Anglicise your name?"
"Our democratic ideal is A Fair Go for All."
One journalist goes to ground for his story,
Returns in country-dark to tup a snaggle-toothed girl,
Standard-issue pinafore tucked beneath against
Rough, exotic scrub. Dry insects in her head,
Redgum veins the sky, she wrestles this hemisphere's
Inverted moon through branches, face no longer aghast
But with a full-cheeked grin. He will remember rolling
In her body's rich smell. Her baby will be born feet-first.

Lysol for personal hygiene. Mum for underarm odour.
Silkynut Hair Remover. Kolynos Dental Cream.
(A South Sea Islander in her grass kilt nods, idly scoops
Fingerfuls of dirt, rubs at her rack of titanium-white teeth.
She spits a gob; the camera cuts; she squats and gushes
Nodding to the sunrise.) Anacin Tablets for difficult days.
Forham's for bleeding gums. Beecham's Pills,
The Vegetable Laxative. Ponds Vanishing Cream.

Tugger sets up pins at City Bowl—piss-stained overalls,
Hand curled like a fern, middle finger taps morse on his
    palm—
Sorts like lightning, beams gravestone teeth to regulars.
Turns up one day, birthday badge on his torn chest:

CPA—*Support Malay Insurgence*. "You're mum's a commo.
On yer way, Tugs—no 'ard feelins." He kept walking,
Where his feet led him. He washed ashore a week later.

Russia builds the Atom Bomb. It's on the radio,
Warming words to critical mass as tea boils.

The family sits side-on to it (sons itch to touch
But father royally dominates dial and black knob,
As he controls the keys to his seagreen Holden);
They eye each others' responses to news reports—
Medical, economic, sporting, the State of Empire—
Not facing directly the scratchy information glowing
From arcane glass tubing and solder-boards
Wireless, neatly boxed in furniture-brown.
A third World War is inevitable. It will be soon.
It will be atomic. It will end civilisation.
Informed Australians are global, optimistic, fecund,
And know we are all going to die. Before that,
They will lose their children to the bright world.
Boom time.

TELEVISION ADVERTISEMENT

a *Yellow Submarine*
Kindersurprise
dense, sparking infonode

crack open its nuclei—
out flower coral shoals
a ripe, sticky *Alien* egg

containing Venus flytraps—
coruscating mouths rise
on looping *Python* stalks

B & H

1.

MIDDLE TAR As defined by Australian Government

DANGER: Government Health WARNING:

risk-taker, go-getter, break the mould,
break the rules, go for the gold,
lighten up, light up,
match the pace,
fly, choose
LIFE
no buts,
beat the odds,
don't lose, jump now,
stand and endure, go for broke,
seek prestige, challenge—eat my smoke

**CIGARETTES CAN SERIOUSLY DAMAGE
YOUR HEALTH**

2.

HIGH TAR As defined by Australian Government

Emerging from his cave of sleep, he found an oblong form that towered from the earth eclipsing the new sun. His peers cowered, but more was expected from him. Tentatively, afraid to appear afraid, he shuffled closer, snorted at the inert thing, then scuffled back, waving to the others. His hand rose towards the flat surface; his fingertips tingled as they crossed that fearful space, and touched. An electric squeal came across the sky, and the monolith turned gold. He leapt away, then in a flash he knew it was all right. Lightning flickered, an aureolan rainbow breathed up from the head of the newly gilt sentinel. Activated by intelligent contact, to instruct and succour. He beckoned, then stood back, as a crowd slowly grew at its base, pelage faces a blurred moving mass of brown-and-orange, the morning sky reflected sun-gold. Behind them, his leadership proven, he held a white bone between his fingers, and pondered the limitless future.

PORSCHE

No bullshit:
It says money.
It means you're the best man.

The car slips down the freeway,
Smooth as sex;
Cool, virile lines;
Low and laid-back;
All comfort,
All power.

Be convinced:
Fast manoeuvres,
Sharp moves,
Four litres
Fucking flies.

It thrusts superiority
In the faces of scum:
The cunts'll only see your arse.

If you're small, it makes you big:
It means you've beaten them.
Porsche means you've won.

WATER

Personalised pharmaceuticals
In neat packets with labels:
Place a half-tile under tongue, 10:30,
Wash down with water;
Drop green caps and white E tab, 1:45,
Wash down with water.
Journey through the bottle—
The chemical looking-glass—
Inject shrink-sealed syringe marked *,
Sniff contents of alfoil ball
(Platinum AmEx for a neat line), 4:00,
Counter dryness in throat with water.
Synthetic dreaming, hypnotically
Awake, warped into nightmare vignettes;
Smoke two Escorts in pack marked Ha
(Not He, that's for next Thursday), 5:45,
Drink plenty of water.

WORLDWIDE

you're a circuit card turbo-charging the exponential
    evolution of our infant Collective Cortex
you're a minor demiurge, an *avatar mythique* from Magic
    the Gathering
you're an interactive schoolgirl
you're an octogenarian Ancient Mariner
you're Bret Easton Ellis talking Star Trek and the bible
you're Scheherazade talking gun control
you're eavesdropping on crash-victim therapy:
    conversational currency loneliness, anger, make it up
you're anonymously prowling, playing temporal hookey
you're violating personal information toggles
you're kissing sleeping strangers, leaving them
    soiled, compromised
you're in the greatest sandbox ever built—but feral
    moggies from the 'hood treat it like cat litter
you're a hypermedia information-storage system
    linking resources, tied to the aggregate
you're a 24-hour shopping channel electrode-wired into
    soft lobes
you're ice-crystals spreading over a cold glass pane,
    doubling every 53 days toward the half-billion
you're loose-weave, now a single sheet, a new Ice Age
you're global harmony in the Great Hive
you're a noose around mankind's collective consciousness
you're a seat in the control room of our frontal cerebrum
you're at the top of the brain stem, catching primal
    synaptic impulses
you're maypoling around the pineal gland
you're a lab rat on an intermittent reinforcement
    schedule
you're downloading *free* images, *free* pornography,
    free information

you're a flea market
you're a Trade Fair
you're a virtual proto-magazine
you're corporate wish-fulfilment
you're the game.

CIRCUITBOARD

The charge
Of thought
And intellect
Passes through structured ether, receiving

The glow
Of insight,
Experience,
In return for the intensity of the outlay.

The ghost
Of awareness,
The mind's electricity,
Traces varying pathways across the board.

The mindfield
Of each reader,
Each reading,
Determines the quality of induction.

The oceans
Of electrons
Catch and swirl
Consciousness in their eddies and flux.

The current
Lights up
What it touches,
Illuminating one route each time through

The maze
Of the grid,
And passes out,
Changed from when it entered.

PROTOZOA

Converging Wealth
in an undersized pond
skins semipermeable
rub against each other
allowing trade, information
exchange through plasma

Liberated Capital
whips through and around
linked nuclei: electrons
travelling at light speed
charge the frosted ether
with a monetary glow

Emerging Markets
without escape velocity
lights dim and unevolved
but people-rich bazaars
asset-enhanced souks
approaching critical mass

Established Economies
extend pseudopodia
eager to gently probe
overcome barriers, flow
into resources, inject
into yielding nuclei

Business Dollars
working from within
for the greater hegemony
units absorb, fuse, blend
munch and excrete
the globe, coalescing

FAMILY FURNITURE DISCOUNTERS

Dave, Dave—no listen.
Dave, boss—listen, no
Listen.
I got it. Okay? Everyone?
Boss. Okay? Okay. It's here
Here somewhere. It's—
A presentation? Well, yep. It's rough.
A bit rough. I'll
I'll talk you through, sketch it
On the OHP. Okay? Picture
This. It's a meadow. Okay . . . Alright
It's a meadow. On film, obviously.
Got that? Yes? It's
Not much of a sketch—but
You get the idea. Yep? Okay.
What?—Oh, they're sheep, Dave.
In the meadow there. You—
You see,
On their flanks are—Yeah.
On their sides. Yep. On the sides of the sheep
Are cards.
Big. Got it? Pinned there. Somehow. Square,
Squarish—see? Well, y'know.
Yeah, guys, rough night, still shakin',
Know where I'm coming from, ha ha.
But—alright—this is it.
On the cards—
Cheap whiteboard, you know the stuff,Do you? Nothing
    fancy,
Keep inside the cheapskate's budget—
Yes, Dave? Boss. Yes?
How? A close-up.
Well, yeah—with a close-up.
So . . . yeah, that's right, that's right.

Yep, got it. Made a note.
Okay? So anyway.
Anyway—on the cards
Are the items,
The selected items—yeah, they're
On a list here somewhere I got faxed from them
    last week.
I mean yesterday.
And the prices. With the numbers—
The numbers are bigger. Right.
Right? So . . . Yep. Lemme just
Just draw it.
An example . . .
A sheep not a cloud, asshole. Fuck you too, Matt.
So—
Like, you get, this:
Modular Lounges Four Niney Nine
Bargain Suites from **Nine Niney Nine**
Tasteful 3-Seater a Tiny Three Senny Nine
Got it, Dave. Yep—but there's more:
Two Leather Chairs a Crazy Two Thirdy Nine
Recliner Rockers Out For Five Niney Nine
And:
Free Coffee Table with Every five hundred
    dollar **Purchase.**
Yep.
Yep. Yep. Yep.
Yeah. Nope. Yep.
Yeah. Yeah but—
Well, they're sheep. I know. In a meadow.
I know. Because—
Because, right?
At the end, the voice-over—
No, no-one in mind right now, Dave,
Could be that weather dickhead from Channel 9—
But the voice, anyway,

Will be. Say. You know. Something like.
You know: Don't be a sheep.
No, not that. But, you know.
Something like:
Follow the herd—Follow the flock.
People will flock.
That sorta thing. Right? Right?
I'll give you fucking prepared, Damien.
Get the idea then guys? Yep? Okay.
Pens down boys and girl.
Yeah, Dave, that's
That's it.
Well, you know—roughly. There's
More to it than that
Obviously, but—
Yes?
Boss?
Sure, no wuckins. I'll just
Pack up here—
No, sure. I'll be across in a sec, I
Have to make a—
Yea, now. Alright.
Not a problem.

PEPSI (AUSTRALIA)

(Well, that's him all over, isn't it. Country Road paisley,
    I bet.
Type that thinks PC stands for Politically Correct. Haha.
Haha. No, me? Me– . . . Mister Armani! Come off it.
    Give me credit for a bit of
Flexibility. Well, not everything. The floral's RL. Bow in
    my pocket's Calvin K. See.)
Alright. Alright. Attention. Please. Everyone.
Thank you, Paul?
David has previewed some of this—so this is new for the
    rest of you, update for him.
The folders in front of you have
Colour-copies of the storyboards, and
Transcripts of the text.
Now, all plug in your laptops—
Alright, *or* notebooks, you 80-gig wanker—
There'll be a short animation, just
To outline where we're going on this.
'Ll fill in the gaps later, naturally.
Inbetweeners. Cleanups. So on.
After all, David
It's Week Two out of six, right?
Thanks—
But no resting on laurels, eh.
So. 'S you can see,
Similar to the US product, but with
Australian flavour, as per
Licensing charter set out by their mother company,
And legislation due to fucking actor's union screws.
So—yes, coming up now . . .
CBD type in YSL or Ralph L swigging one,
Cane farmer guzzling one down, in front of
    burning fields,
Abo in front of Ayers Rock or the Todd or somewhere, et

Cetera. And
Live montage at end—
Ten or twelve seconds—
Several big Aussie faces, the biggest-
Yes, David, they're almost all confirmed now:
Farnham, Blundell, Little, Gunston.
That's quite alright, David. Feel free to break in
Anytime.
So, high profilers all—these and probably others—
Swigging the stuff and
Saying, "IT'S FABULOUS—"
Yeah, I knew some smartarse would say it.
They are *still* bankable faces, gutterboy:
Save your wit for the Target checkout, Paul.
"It's Time" actually was a great campaign—
Pity about the product! Haha—
"IT'S FABULOUS" 'll be better.
Which brings us to promotional strategy.
TV medium saturation starting October
Building up to plateau at end of ratings, all three
    stations, then
Review Feb, March.
Detailed schedule of spots to Jan in your folder. Read it.
Company wouldn't come at royalty deal.
Pity: Stations lap them up. Never mind.
Budget let us choose the spots—
Costs more, but all prime time.
No midnight-to-dawn sheep jewellery, eh, Paul?
Yes, good remind, David:
Summer variation'll drop a couple of faces and
Replace with, prob-
Ably . . . Daddo, JPY, and more—for
The younger, beach set.
Cinema, video—
Not Columbia flicks, Coke owns those bastards.
Video variation (my input from
Our latest round-table, David):

Large, semi-opaque PEPSI and FAB over most of ad
So the trigger-happy fast-forward jocks still get the pitch.
Um—excellent point, David. Although . . .
Alright, just for you I'll mention it next RTM:
If FAB looks too much like TAB on double-speed cue
We'll change it.
It's your sharp mind that's kept you at the top so far,
      David.
Good one.
Right, then—
No, no, no. Hold it. Not now.
Yes, you'll get your chance for Q and A in a couple of
      weeks.
At the moment it'd only
Confuse you, and hold us up—and
You wouldn't want to be seen to be being obstructive
By those that count, would you?
Keep your paperwork, do your homework, and if
      anything occurs
Mention it, politely, next time.
If it can't wait, fax me:
I'm jetting around for the next few days.
Alright. You've heard it. Catch you.
Oh. Lunch?
Um, yes. Yes, certainly, David.
But you remember-
Yes, about two. Okay.
That will give you time enough-?
Yes. Time for me?
Well, I'll just have to pass on the Sambuca.
Alright.
Pardon?
Hahaha. Haha. Haha.
David, you know my place is here.
Two Eye See
Is fine by me.
Wage's enough to keep my tailor in BM's,

And I couldn't keep up with the pace you set, my friend.
Okay. Two it is.
Good one.

THE UNDERGROUND
BANANA CLUB

Shutup, shutup . . .
Order, thank you?
Yes.
Gentlemen? Oh,
I know. Sorry Veronica.
I used "gentlemen" generically.
So is that what you call silence?
 . . . Alright.
As I said, the Banana Club's gone for my pitch in a
    big way;
All that remains-
Yes it *is* a gay dance club and bar. So frigging what!
    Get a life,
Matthew—you fucking breeder.
Sorry, David.
Yes, you too, Matty—let's kiss and make up.
Yeah, outside—but we'll toss to see who bends over first.
Alright, alright, alright:
The Club's signed on the dotted line, and the money's
    up front.
Not bad?
The push is this:
Gay mags, street rags, uni giveaways,
Broadsheets and leaflets with freebie coupons
    scattered around-
The Messenger? Thank you for that input, Paul.
No, really, I think a few gardening pensioners'd liven the
    place up;
They could bring their secateurs for company.
Okay—sorry again, David.
The whole thing hinges, actually (no pun intended),
On the ABC.

If they squash it—which they won't and I'll tell
     you why—
We'll just have to go underground; and that
Mightn't be such a bad thing anyway.
Bananas in Pyjamas are *going* to be Gay Icons—
If they aren't already.
It's a groundswell thing—
As long as we keep just the right side of copyright for
     the moment—
People just need nudging in the right direction.
It could be . . .
I think it could be bloody enormous- . . .
It had to be Matthew, didn't it:
Perhaps those pensioners could bring a chain-saw for
     you, Matty.
Anyway I think
Some of the rest of us can see the potential spinoffs
     from this.
But what's exciting is the approach.
First: my team's contracted that . . . uh,
That local band, what are they called, Ronny? Cartid,
Cantoid, Carotid, or something.
They're gonna do us a gay grunge cover of **Bananas in
     Pyjamas** called
"Coming Down the Stairs" . . . or "Going Down On the-
     " What is it-?
"Take You Unawares." Thank you, Ron.
Anyway, just for this cut they're changing their name to
     the "Teddy Bears."
(If they do well out of it the band'll keep the name and
     do an album.)
Only potential glitch to keep a lid on if nec, is
The kid's drug market link:
If "Chasing Teddy Bears" gets
As popular with under-12s as Chasing the Dragon,
We'll have to walk away from it.
This is why there'll be no pharmaceutical tie-ins:

Even if Vitamins **B1** and **B2** are great in cereal, or as a
    hangover cure—
Too many problems.
But meantime we'll bribe a bit of airplay on the track, get
    it happening as a single, and
Bingo—promotion's free from then on.
Ball's rolling on its own.
Not bad?
Move over Damien—I'm on my way up!
But there's more, Lady and Gents:
What's really *really* exciting is that when Auntie gives
    us approval-
No, not *if*, David: I've done my research.
B1 and **B2** exist only to generate sales—
They're purely and cynically an advertising tool.
What I'm offering the ABC is the way to boost their
    market
Tenfold. And you know how gay culture
Feeds back into popular culture . . .
Oh, they will listen, David:
Companies are buying
Favourable exposure on the ABC
All the time. Did you see Export Australia?
Five-minute prime-time ads for ANZ, James Hardie, and
    Carlton Breweries.
And my client's not asking for anything as crass as free-
    to-air television, or even placements—
All we want is
Juxtaposition.
Give us the right to manipulate their product,
Give them the kickbacks, and get them to
Shift **Bananas** to the 5:45 slot and play the Teddy Bears
    clip before the six o'clock news.
Coupla weeks on, everyone's made the connection.
Good?
And:
And and and:

The even more brilliant bit:
When it all kicks on,
When the track happens,
When the Club and us are rolling in it, and
When the contract's renewed:
A few months down the track . . . right? . . .
A float in the Mardi Gras!
With **B1** co-commentating with the ghost of
   Patrick White!
Alright—David Marr'll have to do.
Yeah, yeah—shutup: gone over time, right?
Okay. End transmission.
But
Not bad, eh?
Not bad.

CICCONE CHICKENS

Thank you, David. Uh. Mhm.
Thank uh you all for uh
Giving me your real time. I don't
I don't get up from R&D
Into the cushy part of the building
That often uh so uh
But I think I might have
Uh something valuable to
Contribute uh mhm–
Oh dear. Did I hear right?
No, David, that's
Uneccesary—I've been called worse.
Damien, is it? Where I come from
Geek means Legend. Geek means God.
Mhm. No I don't dress like you.
Who's this one, David? Matt?
Well, Matthew, thank you for pointing it out.
But, you know . . .
I am the future.
Get used to the smell, earthlings.
If you move away from *me*—Veronica?—you
Retreat from the cutting edge
Of advertising-
So who are you, Paul? A hairdresser?
Feisty bunch, aren't they David.
This the way you treat a guest?
If I'd known, I would have wore a clean t-shirt.
But let's begin, mhm?
You wouldn't get away from your low-tech lounge here,
And visit us in Research, so
Here's what you gotta do:
Plug mobiles into laptops, dial,
Bring up Explorer, . . .
And let's go surfing.

Okay: Ciccone Chickens,
One of the big national fastfood outlets,
Wants a new series of ads,
Tied in with a Web presence.
After last year's "Here, Chick, Chick" campaign
I can see why they switched admen.
(Sorry Veronica, I meant 'men' generically.)
So here's what to do-
I mean, what I *recommend you* do.
(Us basement types gotta know our place, right?
You might get revenge by outsourcing our jobs.)
Ciccone already have a tacky little site on the
      World Wide Web;
Let's find it.
In the URL box near the top
All type http://www.ciccone.com.au
No, two *back*slashes, Matthew.
No, not a comma, a full-stop;
Could you help Damien spell 'au', Veronica?
(And they call *us* nerds.)
Alright. For those who've found it:
The farmyard pics gotta go.
I don't know how cutting edge you wanna be visually—
But giant android chickens
Cannibalising one another with chips and gravy
Is one way to go . . .
Okay, okay—too much too soon.
But we should have a few nifty
Animations and sound files to play
With some Java applets, mhm—
And do away with that HTML link
To the Animal Liberation battery hen site.
Maybe we could get them to invest
In an online game. Costly,
But it builds a loyalty relationship with customers.
A game makes it interactive. And educational:
Free-range chooks could be harder to shoot,

But you get more egg-points.
Something like that.
Also, I'd invest in WebAudit software
To get reports on the background data
Of everyone who hits on the Ciccone site.
This isn't invasive—
No-one kids themselves any more
That companies don't watch their every move on
    the Net.
Newer versions of the package
Promise to track surfers from site to site-
Oh, that shouldn't send shivers down your spine,
    Veronica:
That's marketing.
That's what we're here for—
To snare potential customers,
But let them think they've still got a choice.
Other issues . . . –
You still with me? Matthew?
Yeah, Matthew's found Bianca's Smut Shack.
Um, rather than waste time now,
Come for a visit downstairs sometime
And the boys'll give you a bookmark file
Of all the choice porn sites.
You'll find corporate subscriptions are cheaper
Than paying by the hour to jerk off in your study.
Meantime:
Ciccone Chickens could host other chosen sites:
A CC GIF and link on the CSIRO Page,
Farmers Union, Sydney 2000,
Welcome to Wombat Lake, the Brisbane Bears.
Only problem is
The more mouse clicks on your GIF,
The more you pay.
So to clients it seems to be
Either too costly or a waste of time.
Therefore—last and best—

Search Engines.
It's free to register your site with them,
But amongst half a billion other sites,
Where's your visibility?
Who's going to scroll through 49,000 hits
On the keyword 'chicken'?
And try 'Ciccone', you get
200,000 Madonna sites.
So.
I have some addresses.
The relevant people who run certain Engines
Will gladly accept a fund transfer,
Along a secure line,
To buy the top spots in Search Results.
A paltry $10,000 (pun intended)
Will get your chicken shops position number ten.
That means you're onscreen straight up.
80,000 for number one spot, for six months.
If you're serious about Web presence,
This is the way to go.
But tell CC to get in now:
In a year companies will be bidding those prices
Towards the million.
Well that's about all I've gotta say;
Food for thought, mhm?
Let us know down in R&D
Which way your client goes on this,
And we'll set it up straight away.
I'm outa your faces now—
Yes, Damien, and your nostrils.
Email me
If you don't wanna share the same room
Or hear my voice again.
Just quit the Browser
Before you switch off your mobile to exit the superhighway.
And Matthew:
Stay any longer at the Smut Shack

And David's gonna bill you
For steam-cleaning the carpet.
Engage. I'm gone. Mhm.
See you in the future.

SONAX BUDGET CLASSICAL COMPACT DISCS

Alright, it's the . . .
The what? Oh,
Sonax? Sonax. Yes, I hear.
–Ax? AxAxAx. Okay—got it.
Yes, yes: Sonax. *Sonax*. Jesus. Am I a fucking moron?
Stick to Producing, Julian.
Am I glowing? Or sweating like a pig here? You. You.
Yes, you crawling over masking tape there.
Hump Camera Three later.
Bring that shit over here. Yeah, the whole box.
Oh, thank you sweetheart—you have a gentle touch.
You might dab a bit harder. Harder.
No. No, wipe. You're new here, aren't you? Tip for
    beginners:
You've gotta shag the *floor manager* if you want to get a
    head start around here on   your back.
Just under the eyes a bit more, okay?
No, that's alright—you'll learn.
Get us another Scotch, eh?
Only joking. Joke.
Now, Julian. Julian? Damn it—
I'm waiting! I'm sitting down here under lights—
We don't want Make-up back, do we?
Earth to fucking Control Room! Julian!
Yes! Yes it's the Bitch speaking.
Oh, very important call I'm sure, right in the middle of
    the show.
Executive Director of IMM perhaps?
Bruce from Corporate Affairs discussing the ACTN float
    with you? In your dreams.
Anyway,
Now you're in my ear, dear, at last,
To business:

You cut me short on the last segment: better have
    a good–
How many calls? Shit.
That was their flagship budget stereo I was pushing, too.
Sanity aren't going to like paying for those statistics.
Stuff 'em. It's not my fault. Shithouse product.
No it doesn't *concern* me that Janice got three times the
    callers for all of her   segments just before.
No. No! You *made* me read all that crap off autocue the
    sponsors supplied:"1200X Megadrive Autoquark
    Chrome Foxtails." Jesus!
You can feel those Cable Ladies glazing over—
What's this stuff doing on Interactive *Daytime*
    Shopping anyway?
    . . . You setting me up, Julian?
Fuck off yourself. I'll pull this headgear off and take
    it solo:
Then we'd both lose our jobs, eh?
No you wouldn't—because ads are banned on Cable.
Sure, sure: not for long.
Oh, don't make me laugh! Station Identification?
Ten seconds of that over air and we've *all* lost our jobs.
If it's a Producer's whim and not a national strike
They'd find you in the Yarra with concrete Nikes.
Look. Look. Business time now, alright-?
How many seconds?
Right. Right. Yes. Right.
A caller next? You bastard . . . Yes I– I know,
I know we have to stretch this segment out,
But the last one you gave me on air was psychotic.
    . . . .There's a pattern forming here Julian.
I don't care if twenty other people vetted her.
I know, I know. She was from Toorak, her credit rating
    checked out, she'd made recent Cable purchases.
But did you see what those purchases were?
Purse-sized capsicum spray from Janice's Tuesday
    Lifestyle program.

And swatch handweapons from Guns "R" Us!
Yes I *checked*, Julian–
No time now.
Five seconds? Christ.
God. Hair? Alright. Just feed it to me, asshole.
I'll give you "In your ear," Julian. You were hopeless
No matter which orifice you were in-

*Hello and welcome back to ACTN your Home Shopping
station, and we have more value bargains on your Value
Channel in our new Sound Advice segment right now. It's
a fabulous collection of Compact Discs out through
Sontax Music—Sonax Music—and exclusive to
discerning ACTN Home Shoppers. If you've just bought
your new Sanity 1200X stereo system from us or if you
need to revamp your old CD collection then this set is for
you. Eight Classical Compact Discs, eight Famous
Composers, performed by Internationally Award-winning
Orchestras. Good for dinner parties, relaxing in bed, or
just doing the ironing. And if I open one up you'll see . . .
you'll see they can be tricky to get into which is a very
useful antitheft measure. But take my word that there is
over 17 minutes—indeed, 70 minutes of music on every
disc, which means a total of . . . many hours of listening
pleasure. And what would you expect to pay for such an
attractive collection? I won't keep you guessing. It's not
$200. Not even $100. The cost to members and new
subscribers is just $49.95 (excluding postage and
handling). This is a must for the collector and the beginner
alike. A stunning set. Beautiful composers.*

*And now we'll talk to a caller who's just rung through to
purchase this magnificent Classical collection of CDs.*

*This is . . . Prue, a schoolteacher from the Dandenong
Ranges. Hello Prue?*

*Are you there, Prue? It seems- Ah, Prue. You've certainly
got a value–*

*Well, no: ACTN is a wholly owned Australian subsidiary of
International Media Marketing.*

A- as far I know, Prue, Continental Broadcasting Network is
    actually a local production company–
Well if you're really interested, Prue, a variety of investors
    own IMM.
No, insidious isn't a word I'd–
I'd say we meet demands rather than create unneeded–
This is not advertising, it's Retailing. Of course- Well we
    seem to have lost Prue.
Never mind, what we have now is a series of performances
    from this stunning collection so you can see and hear for
    yourselves what marvellous quality and value you'll be
    getting when you buy this great set. Sit back now and
    listen . . .
Julian! Julian!
When I get–
Oh, Bruce. Bruce, mate.
Hello there, great to hear your voice, didn't know you
    were in the neighbourhood.
That bitch just then, eh? Goddamn ABC reporter
    or something.
So how's the new EO pos–
I said what? No,
That wasn't on air. That–
Yes. No. Yes. No, well, the word "orifice" isn't offensive
    in itself–
No I'm not trying to be-
Yes I can understand the Board's–
If I'd said that. But I didn't–
Never. No, I was cued. That was before. It shouldn't've–
Julian!
Come down here, dear. We've got some
Negotiating
To do.

POWERHOUSEEAST
CONSULTANTS

Hey: Chill, guys.
Hear me out. Yeah, what *he* says.
Thanks, David.
Let me set the table for you:
Convergence objectives.
Yes. To Modernise. Modernise. Try a few new things.
Find the signal in the noise.
To bring this company into the twenty-first century.
I know we're already there, Damien—
But some of us are more There than others
(Much of your thinking here is very '98),
And we all need to be brought through
Into the Now
Together.
Funky business. Totally business. Mojo business.
Okay, jump-cut:
The deal has been done, and we have to–
No—no, now where did you hear that?
No.
I don't talk amounts, but less. Way less.
The figures aren't mission-critical–
Yes, yes: much less than two million—
And over at least 18 months.
So some of you will be seeing a lot more of me.
(And some a little bit less.)
Now let's get back to the bright future–
Alright, Paul: *Windy*, but bright.
Alright, Veronica: *Cold* and windy, but bright.
Alright, Damien: *Raining* and cold and windy—
    but still bright.
I guarantee: you'll be right at home with it.
No, not at home on the dole, Matthew—
Unless you *choose*.

Unless you consistently fail
To meet new, very reasonable base revenue goals.
And employers have an extended duty of care,
To manage the transition out of work.
Our enacted exit strategy
Is one of your many safety nets.
I'm not axing individuals;
I'm not deleting sections—
It's a Service Partnership model.
It's strategic. It's–
No. No, Jay—your Research Officer job is a key position.
No. Really, we beg you to stay!
I'm not going to push you too hard too far too soon:
This is a multiphase installation.
But this company's demographic needs to be re-
      engineered:
To curb f-gender depletion.
Yes, Veronica: more women.
More point-and-click generation, than baby-boomer;
Less Birth of Rock 'n' Roll and more Birth of High-
      Speed Modem.
No, Jay. You're fifty-five? No need to worry at all.
No-one's going to be performance-managed out of
      their job. No.
Boy, some days I wish someone'd ask *me* to retire!
But no such luck.
Sure, systematising your knowledge will mean
      outplacements.
But that's good!
You'll be leaner, meaner and stronger for tomorrow–
Outplacement? No, it's not sacking.
It's de-layering.
It's not forced redundancy.
It's re-tooling the organisation.
No, it's not minimising staff numbers. It's *optimising*.
No, it's not Downsizing.

It's Rightsizing. It's Redimensionalising.
It's overcoming your entrenched paternalism, gentlemen.
It's overthrowing constrictive in-house paradigms.
(Stay at the table with me here.)
Your agency has had a fixed resource base for a
    while now.
Yeah, that's you.
And there's only a given set of competencies.
But times are changing, your client base has changed
    (yes?),
The work is different now (yes?), new technologies
    are bottlenecking-
That's right: 'Bottlenecking.' It's a verb.
Have you heard of a verb, Paul? Verbing is very popular
    these days.
You have a high noise-to-signal ratio, Paul.
You gotta build the pipe to catch the business.
So, let's go liquid.
I want to ask you all:
What are your major projects at the moment?
Uh-huh. Yes, uh-huh.
Okay. Okay.
Fast food franchise: Internet and multiplatform gaming.
Dance clubs: underground press.
Pepsi Australia: multimedia, including streaming video.
    (Hm. Impressive.)
Oh, yes . . . Jewellery retail: television, maybe radio.
Quite a diversity.
Now where's your specific expertise come from?
Uh-huh. Right,
Well, Service Partnering—that's us, that's all of us—
Allows you to extend the surface, to bring in
    outside resources,
As the client organisation, at short notice,
For cutting edge expertise in specialised areas:
Visual, Web interactive, targeted multimedia,
    Intranet, whatever.

A digital strategy.

One small step ahead of the legislation.

(These regulatory bodies don't have teeth anyway, these days.)

Oh yes, I'm sure you're very good at it, Damien.

I know you're fantastic at what you do.

You're broadband beta, right. A high bandwidth guy.

But are you the best?

Yes, that's right. I hear you. You're the best the agency's got.

But we don't know that you're the best they're *going* to get.

Until we find out.

I want you to be the best agency for your clients.

You need to be trending positive.

You need to be ahead of the curve.

If you're adding to the greater good, adding to the Light:

That's your bottom line.

And that's what I'm paid to do. For you.

Transitioning-

I'm sensing some aggressive passivity here.

I'm getting assertive intolerance.

You're harshing me badly, Paul.

That's an old-paradigm question.

That's a fourth-level agenda item;

That's right down there with paperclips and Oc Health & Safety.

That's so very DOS of you.

But hey, be sweet.

Yes, I'm an outsider. A 'guru' from some HR organisation.

But it's the outsider that can see what the in-house advisers,

The back-room boys *can't*.

(Sorry Veronica, I mean 'boys' generically.)

So I'm not only here to help you.

To help you achieve more enabled line management,
To improve timelines, deliverability channels and issues.
But I'm here as the *best* person to be able to help you.
If you're hungry for information . . .
We all are, and I know you are (you've proved that
	to me).
Yes, Matthew: *rav*enous. Very good.
. . . Then I'm your talk-to guy.
I'm your action point.
I'm your info-node.
Are we plugged into the same port on this?
Are we going to joint venture on this?
Okay, just hop into the Intranet-
No, no.
I know we've got a kitchen pinup board already, Paul.
	Funny man.
I mean a PC Intranet.
"*What* Intranet?" (I know you're thinking,
And are about to ask me.) Right question.
When you boot up tomorrow morning, you'll find out.
Oh, and there'll be training in the new Network over the
	next week:
Merely press Accept on the first mail that you'll
	find there-
No, Jay: 'mail.' Email has been mail since circa '97.
And the training times will go straight into your
	Calendars.
You can preference the day yourselves.
I told you we're people-friendly.
And so . . .
Welcome to the Revolution.
The first of many.
The future is this week,
And it's in your diaries already.

WISDOM STATEMENT

The world is richer in associations than in meanings, and it is the part of wisdom to distinguish between the two.
(John Barth)

[Projected Powerpoint animation loop of a chrysalis emerging into a butterfly]

I've been on a course.
And I have a report to give.
Let's call it a Proposal.
All of you know me:
'The Knowledge Manager
Formerly Known as Assistant Librarian.'
But perhaps some of you don't know
That just before I went to Queensland
Our CEO, David, invited me into his office.
David said to me: Stephen,
I don't want the workplace I've got.
He said: I know we're network-established.
I know we're Intranet-implemented.
I know we're remuneration-strategic.
I know we're ecommerce-competitive.
But . . . I want more.
I want a bite out of the future.
I want 2005 now, here.
I said: I've been waiting for this moment.
I said: I knew this day would come.
I said: David, you are now ready
To move to the next stage,
To move to the new work environment.
When I return from the Gold Coast
It will be time to Redimensionalise.
When I return, from Final Training,
We will all be ready.
And, frankly, David,
I said: With this high calibre of staff

We have good mission probability.
And so here I stand
No longer Knowledge Manager
But . . . Director of Intellectual Capital.

So let me lay the deck here,
Let me open my kimono to you
So that you can all read the arc.
This is not extreme whitewater.
This is not adventure careering.
Hip yourself to the concept.

Now, Jenny—you are our new Client Greet and
    Interface Officer–
Yes, you answer the phones.
But you are now a Client Greet and Interface Officer–
Yes, you answer the phones.
But you are the company's Client Greet and
    Interface Officer–
Yes, you answer the phones,
You answer the land lines.
And that will never go out of fashion.
But you are–

Look: what about Terry,
Chief of Information Technology?
Not any more.
We're heavily devolving our C-class.
No CEOs, no Chiefs of anything: too authoritarian.
No more pointy bits in this organisation.
Our culture will be all team-based.
We all went orienteering in the Dandenongs
With the Attachment and Bonding Consultants;
Yes. Oh yes, we are ready.
So Terry is Manager of Information Systems.
(Answerable to the Director of Intellectual Capital.)
No, Terry. This isn't downgrading.
It's an opportunity.

No, Terry. This isn't demotion.
C'mon—stitch it together here.
We're giving you the board to ride the next big wave.
IT is still important. Yes it is.
But we just can't predicate the same synergy on
  cyberhyperbole.
We're way past the Information Age.
And we're moving out of the Knowledge Era.
Soon we'll all be embracing Wisdom Management.
And you can't find that kind of enlightenment
Debugging lines of code
Or wavelength-division multiplexing
Or sniffing the gallium arsenide in your CD-ROMs.

Now. The accountants and lawyers.
Some say we are infested with them.
I say: too many lawyers and accountants
Are never enough.
And if business is temporarily trending negative
Or if there's an unexpected liquidity event,
As part of our new loss mitigation substrategy
They will always be useful as support staff.
After all, lawyers are really glorified clerks
Who always wished they'd done an Arts Degree.
(Sorry, guys—but I've seen those Matisse prints
And framed Writers' Week posters on your office walls.
I've seen those weekend tickets to the Archibald
  shortlist.)
Eventually we will merge Accounting and Legal
And call it Resource and Compliance.
The money guys and the law men
(Sorry, Veronica, I use 'men' generically)
Will be our Resource Allocation Advisers
And our Compliance Advisers.
This is a crucial role now.
The Private Sector Privacy Amendment Bill
Has been passed by federal parliament.
It's your opportunity to be creative.

You need to look at the law as the border
Between East and West Timor
Or Cambodia and Vietnam.
If we make occasional forays over the line,
And not too many civilians are fried,
Then no-one's going to care too much
(Not the government, anyway).
We're the Peacekeepers.
We're the protectors of Democracy
And the Free Market.
So it's the lawyers' opportunity to become the artists
You've always wanted to be, to advise us
How best to collect and cross-reference and use
Customer information—those detailed customer profiles
That we've spent so much time and hard work
Collating and databasing.
(All praise for this goes to Carole,
Our new Demographic Data Mining Officer.)
Our lawyers, our Compliance Advisers—
Specialists in the new regulatory framework—
Will be able to keep our markets loose and happening.
So when we sell so-called private information
To financial institutions and insurance companies
Our customers and shareholders can be satisfied
That we've done it sensitively and lawfully
And to the most reputable highest bidder.

Where are our non-chartered accountants?
On your new business cards it will read
Personal Choice Consultant.

Who are our Human Resource staff?
Yes. Yes. Yes. There. And there.
Gosh, you're everywhere.
Well, you of all people know:
Employees are not just a resource,
They're 120% of the value of the business,
They're not our commodities, they're our Wisdom.

So, Pasquilina, you are our new
Manager of People Processes.
Olive (Here? Yes?): Culture Team Leader
Overseen by your line manager, Murray,
     Head of Enhancement of Human Capital
(And responsible to the Director of Intellectual Capital).

Well, that's the plus-or-minus gamut.
As you can see, it's not just new names
But new ways of sharing,
New ways of processing systems,
New impactful ways of partnering and leveraging.

Thank you for hearing.
Please process this.
Nibble on it during the week.
David needs to be thanked for his vision,
For shaking us awake into 05.
If any of you have issues with this
See one of us on the Executive Board
(Yes, Veronica: Executive/Executrix, whatever.)
And we can negotiate you
Into the same sensibility domain as the rest of us.
'Gentle repurposing,'
Our new Retention and Growth Manager might say.

No, don't point them at me right now.
I'm straight off to a communications satellite launch,
Just before the gas and metal mining conference.
Resist the urge to fax me in my shuttle.
I'll be tied up next few nights
With live feeds of the MicroSoft trials.

Until my next return, then, young Jedi Knights:
Remember that what we understand we control,
And wisdom is back in fashion.
Further questions, I'll calendar you soon.
Thanks,
And enjoy the ride.

ACKNOWLEDGEMENTS

Grateful acknowledgement is made to the editors of the publications in which some of these poems first appeared.

The Accounting, Auditing and Accountability Journal,
The Adelaide Review, *Antipodes* (American Association of Australian Literary Studies), *The Australian,* 5UV Writers' Radio, various *Friendly Street Readers,* *Galloping On,* *Hobo, Imago, Island, Lexicon, Overland, The Perfect Diary,* Poetry of the People: North Shore FM, SA Writers' Theatre, *Sleeping Under a Grand Piano: Ten South Australian Poets* (Ginninderra Press), *Southern Review, Streetwords* (Adelaide buses), *The University Readings, Vatra* (Romania).